ETHICAL DATA USE

JO ANGELA OEHRLI

Published in the United States of America by Cherry Lake Publishing
Ann Arbor, Michigan
www.cherrylakepublishing.com

Series Adviser: Kristin Fontichiaro

Photo Credits: Cover and page 1, ©ESB Professional/Shutterstock; page 5, ©Monkey Business Images/Shutterstock; page 6, ©wavebreakmedia/Shutterstock; page 9, ©carballo/Shutterstock; page 13, ©Iakov Filimonov/Shutterstock; page 14, ©Jacob Lund/Shutterstock; pages 16 and 19, ©Andrey_Popov/Shutterstock; page 20, ©Minerva Studio/Shutterstock; page 22, ©Constantine Pankin/Shutterstock; page 24, ©gpointstudio/Shutterstock; page 27, ©karelnoppe/Shutterstock; page 28, ©Linda Parton/Shutterstock

Library of Congress Cataloging-in-Publication Data has been filed and is available at catalog.loc.gov

Cherry Lake Publishing would like to acknowledge the work of the Partnership for 21st Century Learning.
Please visit *www.p21.org* for more information.

Printed in the United States of America
Corporate Graphics

ABOUT THE AUTHOR

Jo Angela Oehrli is a former high school and middle school teacher who helps students find information on a wide range of topics as a librarian at the University of Michigan Libraries. In 2017, she won the American Library Association's Library Instruction Round Table's Librarian Recognition Award.

TABLE OF CONTENTS

What Is Data? What Are Ethics?

Data is everywhere. It's the number of times you are absent in class. It's the number of sunny days per year. It's the results of surveys and **polls**. Data is information. It often comes in the form of numbers. When we apply math to data, we end up with **statistics**.

What are ethics? You can think of ethics as the belief system that influences our behavior. Ethics are the reasons why we create the laws and rules that we have in our culture. For example, our society believes that it is unfair to steal others' work and present it as our own. As a result, we punish people who cheat. We rely on honesty, so we ask people to tell the truth. In most cases, it is easy to identify the ethics that a culture, a country, or a community values. Also, each person has his or her own personal set of ethics. Ethics can be personal promises that you make to yourself

You should always keep ethics in mind while gathering data for a class presentation or any other school project.

that help you act like a better person. For example, maybe you think you should always help people in need. Or maybe you always do your best to treat all people equally.

When we think of ethics, we might not immediately think about how they relate to data and statistics. However, ethics are a very important part of using data. Whether you are using data as evidence in a **persuasive** paper at school or statistics to back up an argument with your brother, you should represent your side of the story fairly. Ethical data use also helps you make stronger arguments. When people know they can trust your presentation of the facts,

Ethics help shape a society's legal system.

they are more likely to see your side of an issue. It is very easy to brush away a point of view that is not based on ethical or true data.

This book will help you understand how to use data ethically. It will provide you with some ways to consider whether the data you might be using has been honestly presented to you. This will help you think about whether you should present it to someone else. You will find that there are general "rules of thumb" to follow when you see statistics. Doing this will allow you to feel comfortable using the data you find.

Trustworthy Data

You know that the books in your school library and the assignments you read in class are most likely trustworthy sources. They were edited by professional editors, produced by reliable publishers, and selected by your teacher or librarian. The work of these professionals helps you feel confident about what you read.

In the real world, we can't always make the same assumptions. Sometimes, information online, in social media, or in print can be misleading or false. Sometimes, authors make mistakes or have incomplete information. Sadly, some writers also lie, mislead, or share only limited information to try to persuade readers to believe certain things.

Learning some strategies for ethically using and discussing data and statistics can make you a better student and citizen.

Finding the Right Data

Before you even consider using data or statistics, you have to find them. There's a lot of data out there. How will you decide where to find the best data? If you use your own ethical **principles**, you will find better data and make a stronger case for your position in an argument.

Some people don't even bother to look for data when they are making arguments. They just make up numbers! There are many Web sites and organizations devoted to making up fake statistics.

Other people make guesses or predictions that aren't based on real information. Ethical data users demand that those who gather statistics "show their work." We'll talk more later about strategies to discover whether a statistic is accurate and should be used.

When you search for data online, you have to choose your sources carefully.

If you search for data from trustworthy sources only, it is less likely that you will be tempted to use data that was unethically created. When you want to know something, you might open a search tool like Google or Bing and start typing in questions. However, not every result will contain ethical data. You should look for Web sites and organizations that clearly explain how they collect data. These organizations make every effort to be honest and transparent. When you read how they've collected their data, you can decide for yourself if their methods were ethical.

The U.S. Census Bureau's American Fact Finder is one example of a good online source for reliable data. Find it at *https://factfinder.census.gov.*

Later in this book, you'll learn more about ethical practices to look out for when you are examining data. There are several well-known organizations that collect trustworthy data. Many of them are run by the U.S. government. Others are private groups with a long history of providing reliable, truthful information. Here are just a few:

- U.S. Census Bureau (*www.census.gov*)
- U.S. Bureau of Justice Statistics (*www.bjs.gov*)
- U.S. Bureau of Transportation Statistics (*www.bts.gov*)

- U.S. Bureau of Labor Statistics (*www.bls.gov*)

- U.S. Geological Survey (*www.usgs.gov*)

- National Center for Education Statistics (*https://nces.ed.gov*)

- Local state and city government Web sites

- Pew Research Center (*www.pewresearch.org*)

- World Health Organization (*www.who.int/gho/en*)

- The World Bank Open Data (*http://data.worldbank.org*)

Many of these organizations are responsible to the people they serve. For example, government Web sites (look for sites that end in *.gov*) are almost always trustworthy. They have a responsibility to obtain and **analyze** data ethically. Look for your information on these sites, and you are more likely to find ethical data.

Rule of Thumb

Search carefully to find trustworthy data. Always consider the source you are getting your data from.

Collecting Data Ethically

There are a lot of ways that people can collect data. Here are some examples:

- They can ask people questions in an interview.
- They can conduct a survey or poll.
- They can ask questions of a representative group of people in a sample survey. People who take a sample survey must be chosen randomly. For example, a random sample survey may ask questions of one in every five female college students at a particular school. The results would then be used to make a claim about all of the female students at the school. Random sample surveys are often used when there is a large group being studied. This is because it would be very difficult to ask every single person.

Conducting a survey in person is just one way of collecting data about people.

- They can watch something happen, including watching something online, and then report what happens as an observation.
- They can design and carry out an experiment and then measure the results.
- They can collect information that was not originally meant to be data and analyze it for patterns.
- They can reuse data collected by other people in new ways.

Each of these methods can be affected by ethics in different

Ethical researchers always take a lot of notes and keep careful records of their plans.

ways. You have to know the rules that apply to each step in the collection process and decide whether the researchers who gathered the data followed them correctly.

Step 1: Pre-Data Collection

Ethical researchers do many things to make sure that their data is honest and reliable even before they start collecting it.

- They plan their questions in advance so everyone is asked the same ones. They also decide how answers will be written down. For example, will the question say, "Do you have pets? Yes or no?" or "Name the pets you have." Different questions will provide different answers! They also decide how they will collect data. A survey? An interview? Through observation? Some other method?

- If they are collecting data about people, they ask permission first. It is unfair, in most cases, to study someone without their knowledge or permission. This is part of what is called **informed consent**.

- In addition, they tell the people they studied what the collected data will be used for. If someone disagrees with the purpose of the data, they can refuse to participate in the collection process. This is another part of informed consent.

If someone is informed, they are aware that something is happening to them. If they consent to something, it means that they agree to participate. Ethical research also requires that

Rules of Thumb

- *Only use data that was collected ethically.*
- *Don't choose data just because it supports your argument.*
- *Always **cite** your data!*

To ethically collect data through an online survey, researchers have to make sure that people can only respond one time.

anyone under 18 years old must receive permission from a parent or guardian before they can take part in that research.

Step 2: Collecting the Data

During the data collection process, a researcher has to make sure that she gathers data ethically. This means a few things:

- She didn't hurt any people or animals in the data collection process. Researchers should not cause physical harm or emotional pain to the people they work with.

- She tries very hard to stick to her data collection plan. If something changes, she writes down her reason for changing the plan. She also makes sure to think about this change when analyzing the data later on.
- She doesn't invent or make up data.
- She stores her data in safe places and makes backup copies. This protects the data from being stolen, deleted, or changed without her knowledge.

Collecting data can be boring, repetitive, and time-consuming. Professional researchers might have to measure hundreds, thousands, or even millions of items. In such cases, it can be easy to get distracted and make a mistake. It can even get so boring that some researchers start making up their data.

Ethical researchers try not to do any harm while collecting their data. They also try to collect their data honestly. They keep track of how they collected their data and communicate their processes to the people who will use their data. For example, a researcher might write that she randomly picked 20 percent of smokers in a large Midwestern city area and asked them, with their consent, "Have you ever tried to quit smoking?" A good researcher will clearly explain how she identified whom to interview and how to get information from them (interview, survey, etc.). She will even include her original questions in her report.

Step 3: Analyzing the Data

Now that the researcher has some data, what does she do with it? She analyzes it! That means that she sorts through all of the information she has, adding up answers when they can be counted and finding patterns in what people have said.

- Sometimes, knowing the identity of who gave information can bias or influence the researcher. So if the researcher collected the names of those who completed a survey, for example, she should make a copy of the answers with the names removed. Only then should she analyze the data.

- She applies mathematical principles to draw conclusions from the data. For example, how many smokers in the previously mentioned study about smoking tried to quit? She might count up the number of quitters and compare them to those who refused to quit and those who wanted to quit but failed. If she asked how many people lived in the household, she might calculate the average. After doing

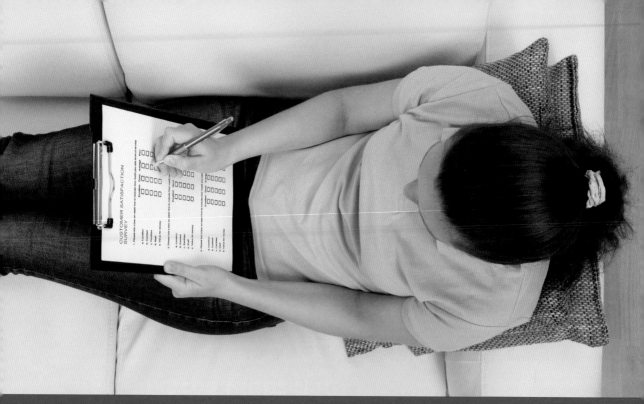

If you want people to take a survey, think carefully about whether you need their name on it. Sometimes, people give more honest answers when they are anonymous.

math calculations like these, she can start to see patterns: Did more than half quit? Do most households have more than two people in them? That will help her understand what the data is telling her.

- She checks her work to make sure her math and conclusions are accurate. An ethical researcher knows that other people will probably use her research, so she wants to be sure she doesn't make any mistakes.

- If there was any change made during the process of collecting data, she explains the change and considers it in

Carefully checking work is an important part of all data analysis.

her analysis. For example, maybe the smoking study started by asking both male and female smokers but later in the survey only asked men. A good researcher would make clear why there was a change. She would sort out male data from female data to also make sure it didn't have an impact on her results.

- If the researcher has permission, she will share her results in a way that doesn't reveal personal information about her research subjects. This helps other researchers learn from what she has figured out.

Using data can be a very powerful method of supporting an argument. But if the information you use was not analyzed correctly or ethically, your argument won't be as strong. Some unethical researchers will remove data if it doesn't fit the claim they are trying to make. Good researchers explain how they came up with the statistics they found. This will make you feel more confident about their conclusions.

Data can be powerful when you are presenting an idea or point of view. If you have an overwhelming statistic that proves school days should last from 10:00 a.m. to 5:00 p.m. every day, that would go a long way to convince parents and school officials to change the school schedule. But if no one knows how you came to that conclusion, they will question your argument. They might think you are just making things up so you can sleep in! Did you just ask the students in your school? Or did you find a research study with quality data? For example, maybe a group of students went to school from 7:00 a.m. to 3:00 p.m. for one year and were then given a test. The next year, the same students went to school from 10:00 a.m. to 5:00 p.m. They took another test, and the results were compared to the previous one. Maybe this comparison was done using a lot of students in multiple parts of the country. Using data like this makes for a stronger argument.

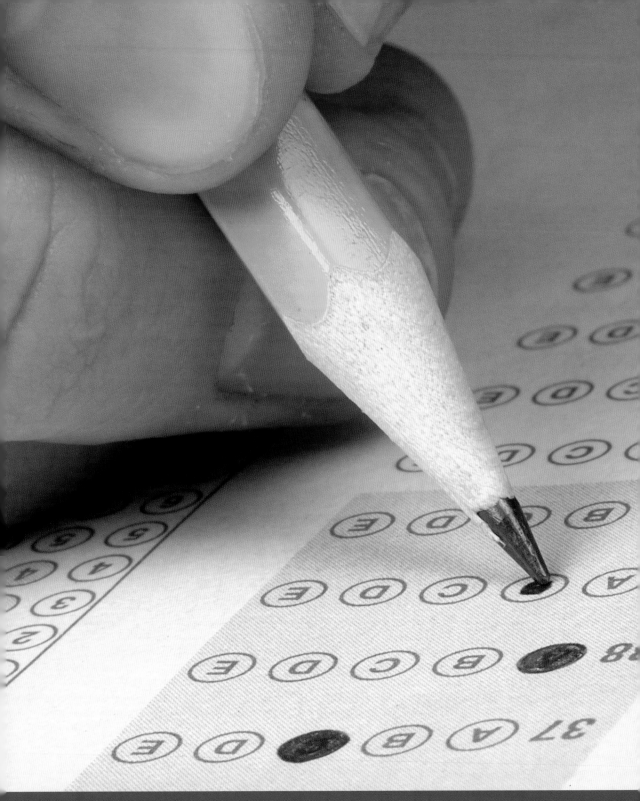

Most students take standardized tests. What would be some ethical ways of using student test data? What would be some unethical ways?

Avoiding Ethical Mistakes with Data

Even when data comes from an accurate source, there are some other factors to think about when using data ethically. Let's look at some examples of how we can accidentally mislead others when we don't think enough about the data in front of us. Let's say you want to figure out how the cost of living has changed over the years. Some people might use comparisons to show how things have changed. For example, they might compare the cost of a loaf of bread. After searching the Internet, they learn that the average cost of a loaf of bread in 1986 was 55 cents. They might then go to the grocery store and see that a loaf of bread costs $1.38. They see that there's a difference of 83 cents between the two prices. That's a 151 percent increase! Maybe grocery stores are charging too much for bread these days!

There are many factors that could affect the change in bread prices over time.

Or maybe they aren't. There could be many reasons for the difference in price. For example, there are a lot of different kinds of bread today. What kinds of bread were sold all those years ago? Also, which grocery store was used? Where was it located? Prices for different items can change a lot from store to store and region to region.

Another factor that influences prices is **inflation**. This means things naturally cost more now than they used to! The Bureau of Labor Statistics' Inflation Calculator describes the value of something in the past compared to today's value. It shows that 55 cents in 1986 is worth $1.22 today (see *https://data.bls.gov/cgi-bin /cpicalc.pl*). That's a lot closer to $1.38 than we originally thought.

Once you have decided to use data, be sure to cite your sources. Find out where your numbers come from, and do the best you can to find the original source of the statistics. Cite that original source if you can, rather than citing an article or book that reproduces the data. If someone has questions or if they want to use the data for their own arguments, they will know where to find it.

What Does It All Mean?

Even if you are an ethical data user, you have to watch out for people who are not. Use your data knowledge to avoid becoming a victim of unethical data users or accidentally contributing to unethical data collection.

For example, there are many Web sites that gather data from their users without consent. Or they might provide some sort of benefit or incentive, such as a coupon or unlocking of bonus levels in a game, if people answer a survey. Even if those Web sites ask really interesting questions and get a lot of answers to their surveys, is their data collected ethically? There are some really big problems with this kind of information.

- You probably don't know who answered the questions. It could be anyone! For example, if a question was more

Always think twice before filling out a survey online, even if it offers a good reward.

focused on teenage behavior, how would you know that only teenagers answered? It is hard to confirm the age, gender, or other identity features of someone who is responding to an online survey.

- What if the same person answered one question multiple times? That person could really influence the results by giving the same answer over and over.

- Maybe that person didn't answer honestly. Maybe they just wanted the coupon. How would you know?

After being misled by government officials who used data unethically, residents of Flint, Michigan, had to rely on bottled water deliveries for drinking water.

Flint Water Crisis

Since 2014, the people of Flint, Michigan, have struggled to get clean drinking water. Some of the city's residents collected data showing that there were significant levels of lead in the local drinking water. However, they received messages from several public officials stating that there wasn't a problem. A Michigan Department of Environmental Quality spokesperson told Michigan Public Radio, "Anyone who is concerned about lead in the drinking water in Flint can relax." This spokesperson reported that 170 Flint homes were tested for lead and that there was no significant problem.

But there was a big problem. Soon, it was revealed that many trusted people in the community had known there was a problem with the water. However, they had not reported it. One research team discovered that 40 percent of Flint homes had lead in their water. Putting lead in a human body can result in a number of health problems. Members of the community were outraged. Data presented to them by people they trusted, including a video made by their mayor showing him drinking Flint's water, could not be believed.

Because data was used unethically, the city's local government and other organizations have made themselves appear untrustworthy. It will be difficult for Flint residents to trust their government officials again.

Always be careful which Web sites you visit and what you click on while you're there. You don't want to accidentally give data away to unethical people. You should also avoid participating in surveys that use poor methods. You don't want to help unethical data spread any farther than it already has!

Data has a powerful influence in our lives. We use it to make decisions about everything from where we want to live to whom we want to vote for in an election. Using reliable, ethically collected data will help you make good decisions. It will also help you present your views to others. People will know that they can trust the things you are telling them, and you will get the satisfaction of making a strong argument. Keep practicing and learning. Before long, you will be a master of using data!

For More Information

BOOKS

Colby, Jennifer. *Data in Arguments*. Ann Arbor, MI: Cherry Lake Publishing, 2018.

Oehrli, Jo Angela. *Statistics and Data Comprehension*. Ann Arbor, MI: Cherry Lake Publishing, 2018.

WEB SITES

American FactFinder
https://factfinder.census.gov/faces/nav/jsf/pages/index.xhtml
This tool from the U.S. Census Bureau offers a wide variety of trustworthy data.

Bureau of Labor Statistics—Occupational Outlook Handbook
www.bls.gov/ooh
This U.S. government Web site has plenty of reliable data about careers and the economy in the United States.

Pew Research Center
www.pewresearch.org
This organization collects data on a wide variety of topics, from politics to science.

GLOSSARY

analyze (AN-uh-lize) to examine something in order to understand it better

cite (SITE) to use and give credit to someone else's work

inflation (in-FLAY-shuhn) the gradual rise of prices in an economy

informed consent (in-FORMD kuhn-SENT) permission to do something that is given by someone who is aware of the details of the situation

persuasive (pur-SWAY-suv) trying to convince an audience of a certain viewpoint

polls (POLZ) surveys of people's opinions or beliefs

principles (PRIN-suh-puhlz) basic facts, laws, or beliefs

statistics (stuh-TIS-tiks) facts or pieces of information taken from larger studies

INDEX